HORSES AND HORSE-DRAWN VEHICLES

A Pictorial Archive

Selected and Arranged by
CAROL BELANGER GRAFTON

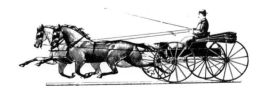

Dover Publications, Inc.
New York

Bibliographical Note

Horses and Horse-Drawn Vehicles: A Pictorial Archive is a new work, first published by Dover Publications, Inc., in 1994.

DOVER *Pictorial Archive* SERIES

Library of Congress Cataloging-in-Publication Data

Grafton, Carol Belanger.
    Horses and horse-drawn vehicles : a pictorial archive / selected and arranged by Carol Belanger Grafton.
        p.   cm. — (Dover pictorial archive series)
    ISBN 0-486-27923-5 (pbk.)
    1. Horses in art.   2. Horse-drawn vehicles in art.   3. Drawing—19th century. I. Title. II. Series.
NC783.8.H65G73   1994
745.4—dc20
                                                  93-44556
                                                    CIP

Manufactured in the United States of America
Dover Publications, Inc., 31 East 2nd Street, Mineola, N.Y. 11501

Publisher's Note

The beauty and expressiveness of the horse's body, the grace of its movements, its combination of delicacy and power in equal parts, its historical role in assisting man in conquering nature, geography and his fellows—these are the subjects of this book. In over 800 pictures culled from a variety of sources, mostly nineteenth-century, the horse emerges not only as a sort of icon, but as an index to human history and perception throughout the ages.

The book is divided into 13 parts, each devoted to a given context in which horses have lived or served. It includes great illustrations (several by Frederic Remington), horse portrait prints, equestrian graphic designs and lovely silhouettes. Horsy persons will especially appreciate the section "Equipment and Accessories," which ranges from everyday types of horseshoe to the ancient and the exotic.

Despite the variety of graphic media represented, all the illustrations will reproduce easily for any printing or design project. They are also ideal for beginning artists who wish to master the contours of the horse, which is depicted here at every conceivable angle.

Contents

THE PASSING OF
THE HORSE
NO FURTHER USE
FOR HIM.
SEE OUR
STAND AT
THE
SHOW.

OBJETS D'ART CURIOSITÉ

W. A. Rogers.

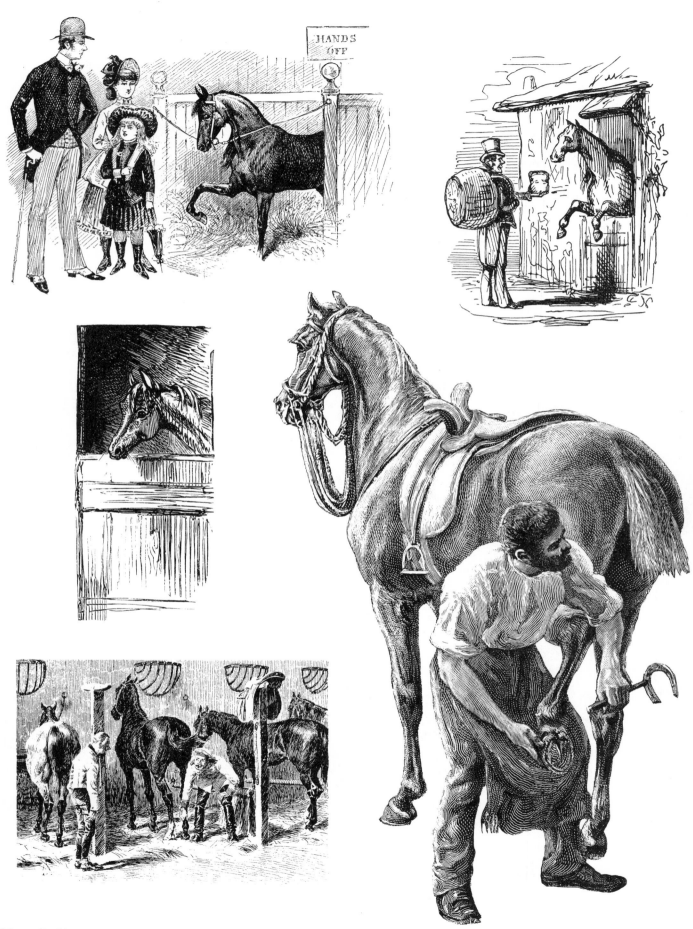

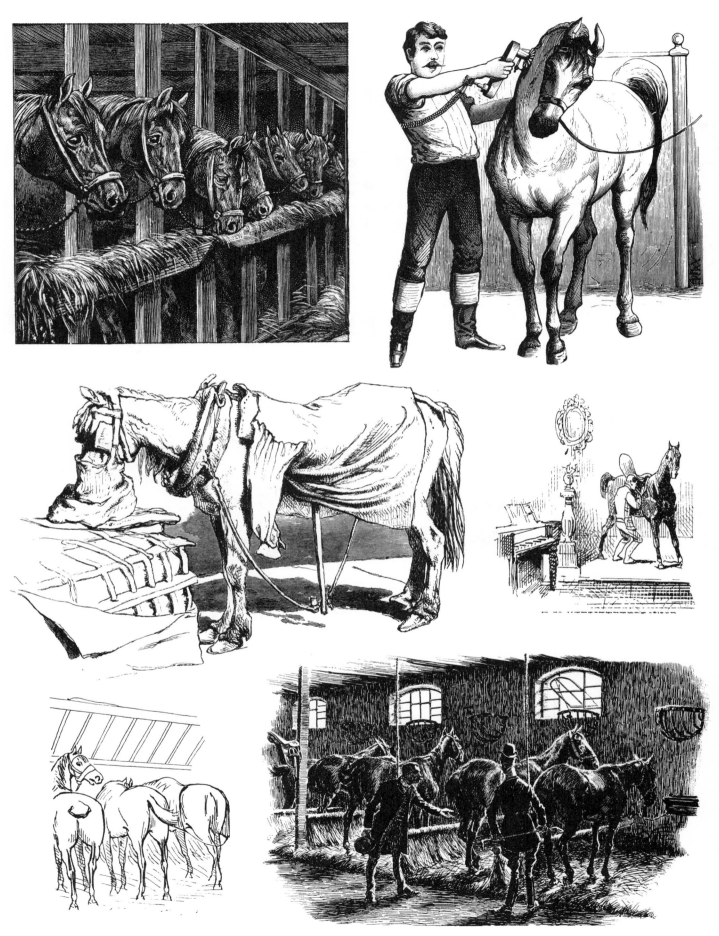

Fourteenth-century War Saddle

Iron Spanish Spur

Viking Stirrup

Standing Martingale

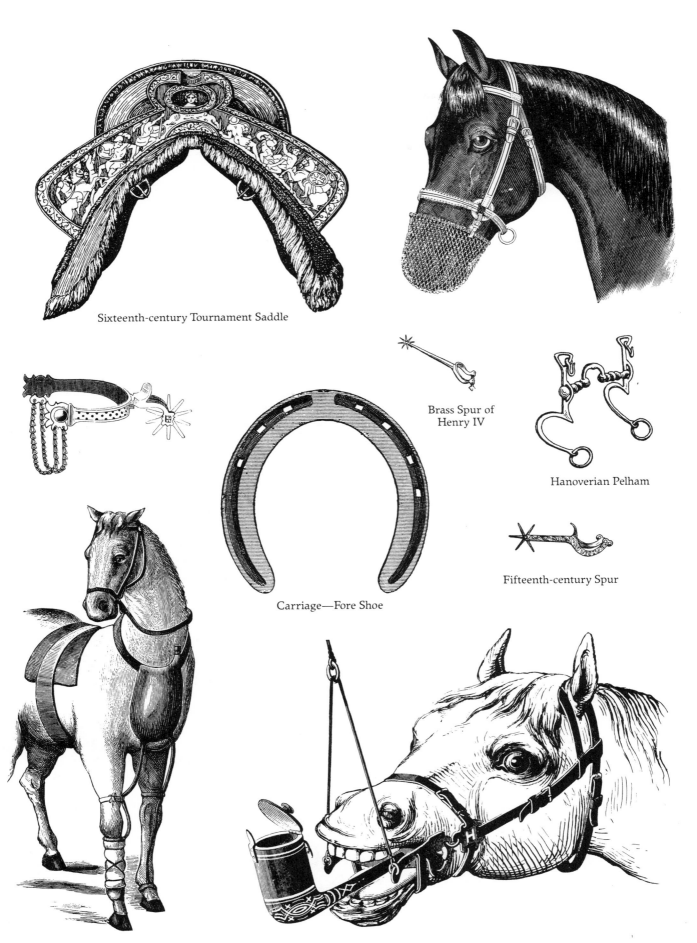

Sixteenth-century Tournament Saddle

Brass Spur of
Henry IV

Hanoverian Pelham

Carriage—Fore Shoe

Fifteenth-century Spur

Modern Arab Saddle

Common Saddle of Fifteenth Century

Fifteenth-century Spur

Primitive Greek
Prick Spur

Mane and Tail Comb

Heavy Horse—Fore Shoe,
Toe-piece and Calkins

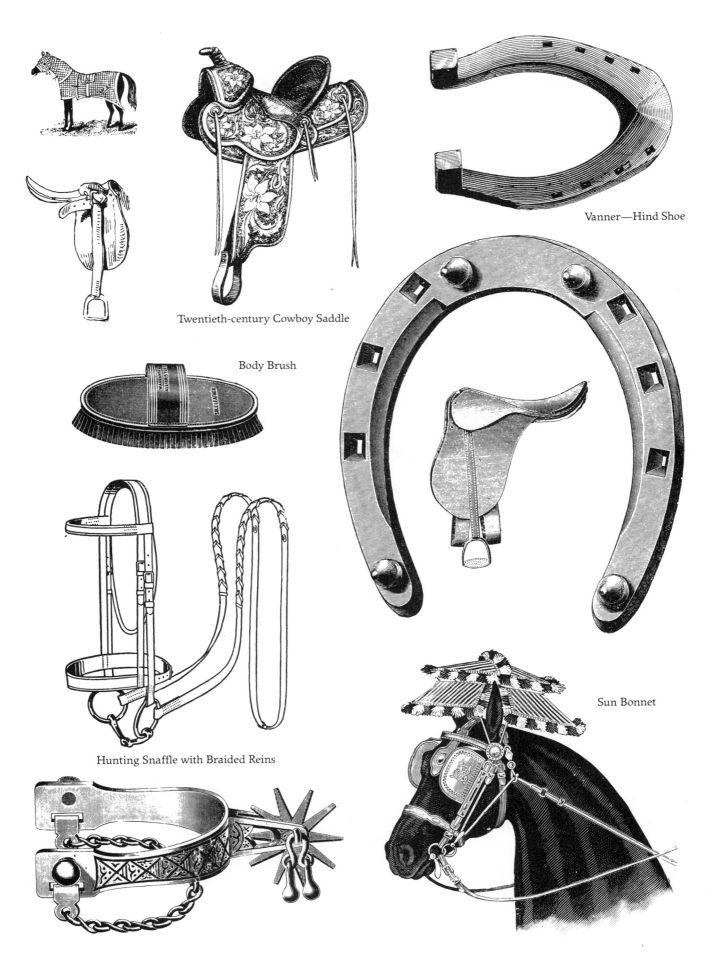

Vanner—Hind Shoe

Twentieth-century Cowboy Saddle

Body Brush

Hunting Snaffle with Braided Reins

Sun Bonnet

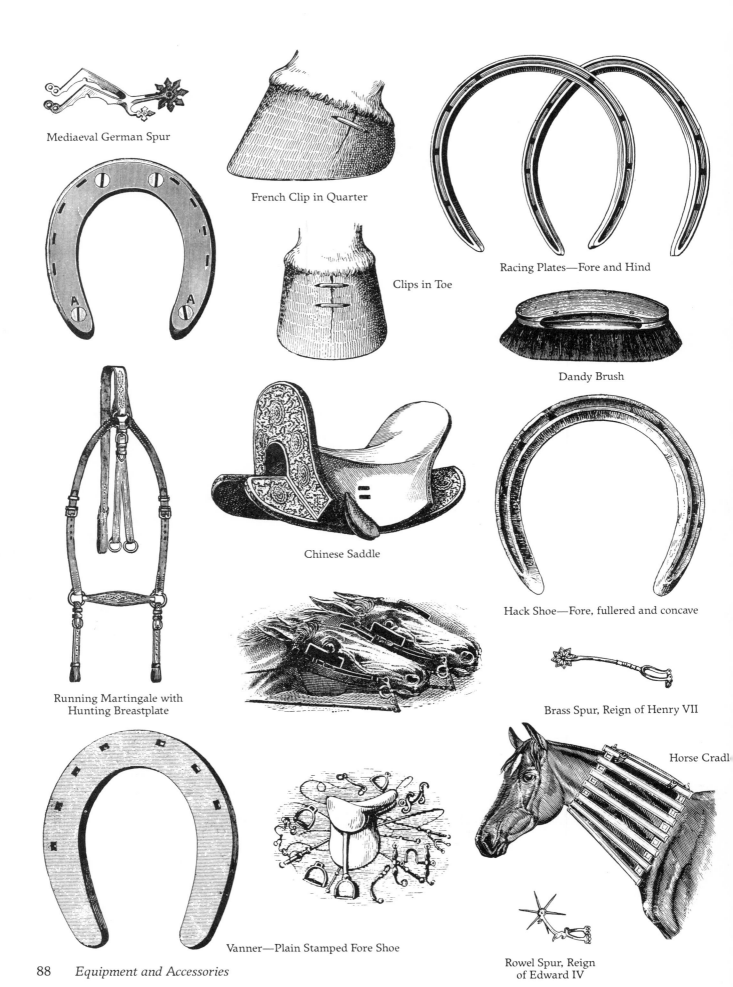

Mediaeval German Spur

French Clip in Quarter

Clips in Toe

Racing Plates—Fore and Hind

Dandy Brush

Running Martingale with
Hunting Breastplate

Chinese Saddle

Hack Shoe—Fore, fullered and concave

Brass Spur, Reign of Henry VII

Horse Cradl

Vanner—Plain Stamped Fore Shoe

Rowel Spur, Reign
of Edward IV

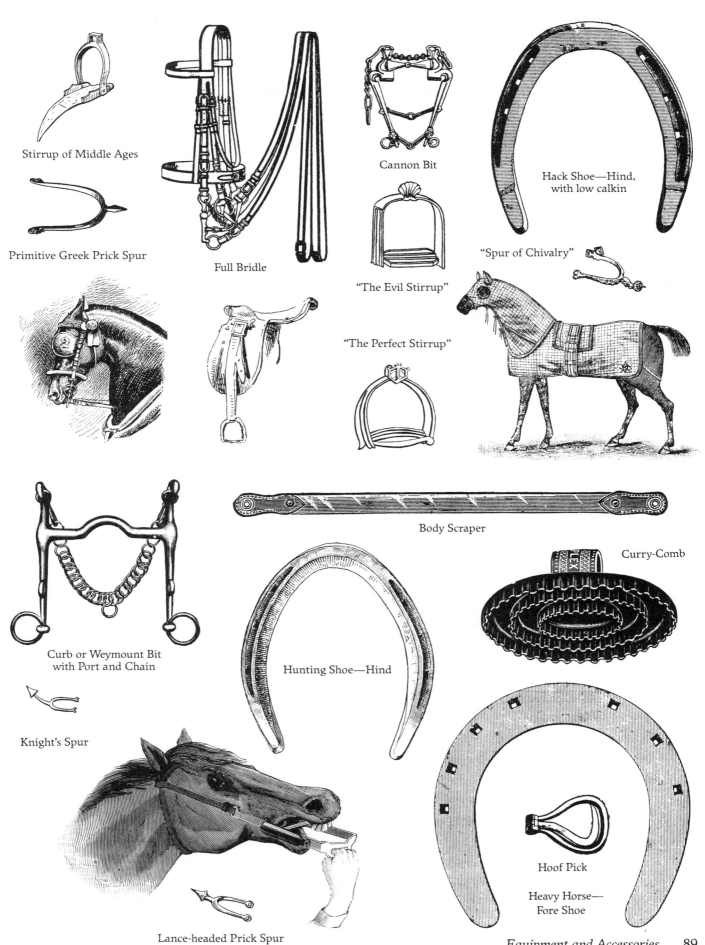

Stirrup of Middle Ages

Primitive Greek Prick Spur

Full Bridle

Cannon Bit

"The Evil Stirrup"

"The Perfect Stirrup"

Hack Shoe—Hind, with low calkin

"Spur of Chivalry"

Curb or Weymount Bit with Port and Chain

Knight's Spur

Body Scraper

Hunting Shoe—Hind

Curry-Comb

Hoof Pick

Heavy Horse— Fore Shoe

Lance-headed Prick Spur

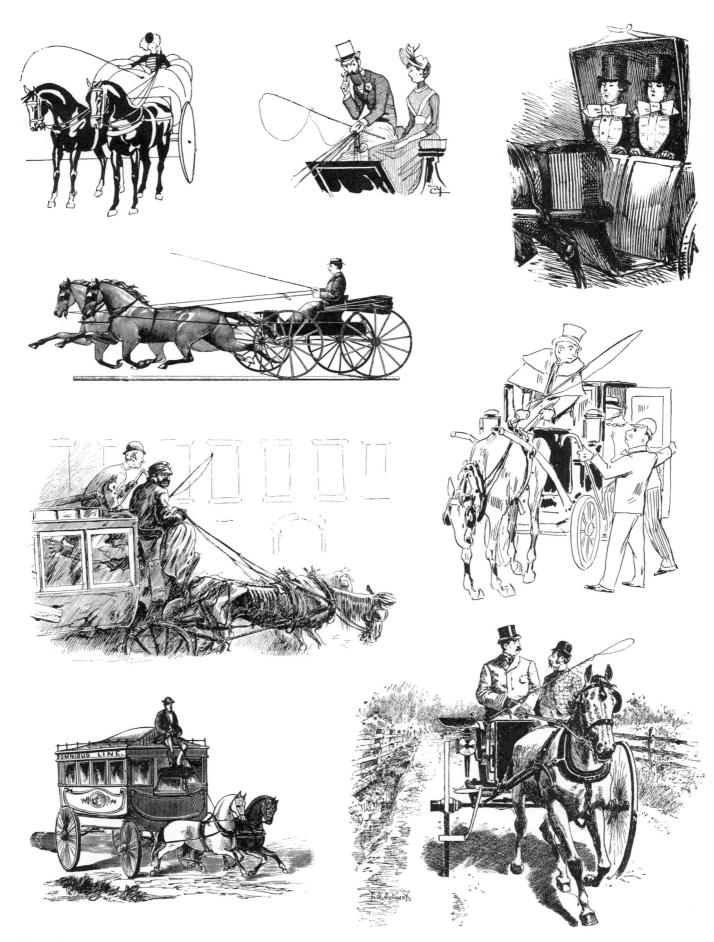

Carriages and Other Horse-Drawn Vehicles

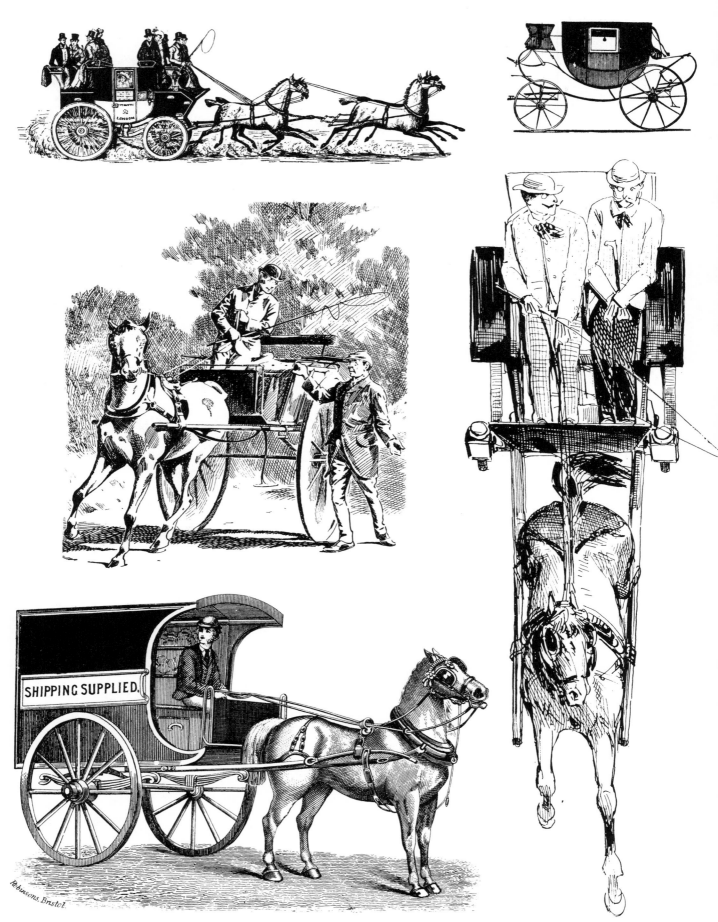

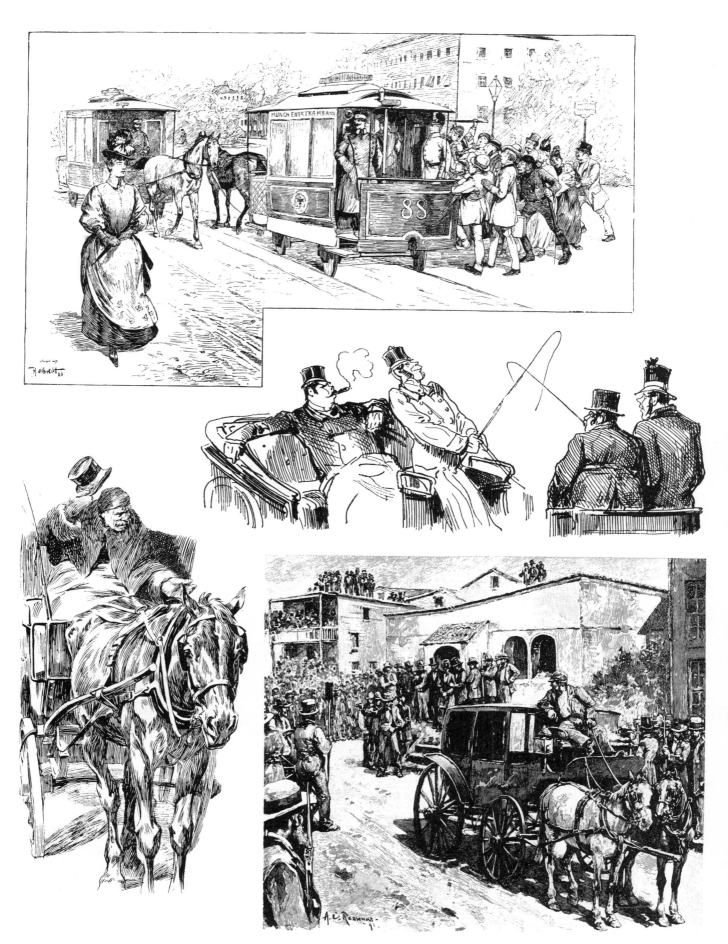

Carriages and Other Horse-Drawn Vehicles

PETRI & PELS.N.Y.

110   *Carriages and Other Horse-Drawn Vehicles*

Carriages and Other Horse-Drawn Vehicles

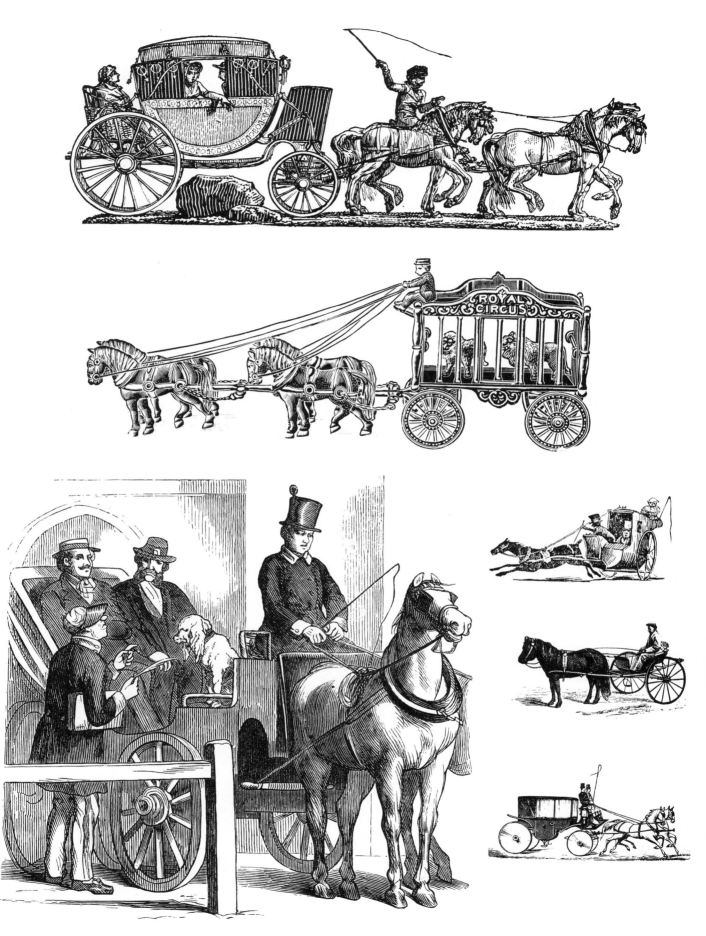